Nature's
BELIEVE IT OR NOT
plants and animals

by Jeff Tichelar

First Edition © 2025

Milk & Honey Ministries
Bible Truth in Prophecy
5500 E. 45th St N, Bel Aire, KS 67220
www.bibletipnow.org

Library of Congress Control Number: 2025906024
ISBN No: 9798218616793

The proceeds from the sale of this book
go toward missions projects
and it is dedicated in loving memory
to my parents, Clayton & Shirley Tichelar.

Table of Contents

Those who live at the ends
of the earth stand in awe
of Your wonders.
From where the sun rises
to where it sets, You
inspire shouts of joy.

Psalm 65:8 (NLT)

EVOLUTION
DOES
NOT
WORK

...and cannot account for what we see in nature!

- 1. If evolution were true – we could expect animals to be more similar than different.
- 2. We would NOT expect the SPECTACULAR variety of lifeforms, fully functional and complex that exist all over this planet.
- 3. There is nothing evolving today! And NO evidence that anything ever evolved, the so-called "MISSING LINKS," are still missing.
- 4. There is <u>NO MECHANISM</u> TO GIVE LIFE TO lifeless chemicals or matter. And NO <u>MECHANISM</u> to add NEW information to DNA.
- 5. No answer to the problem of "IRREDUCIBLE COMPLEXITY." Vital organs and cells that <u>MUST</u> be fully functional from the start.
- 6. NO EXPLANATION for REPRODUCTION! The need for two compatible (but unique) life forms to appear together at the right time (before death) to reproduce – repeated MILLIONS OF TIMES consistent with the vast array of species.

Note to my Readers:

Thank you for taking the TIME to read this book! You will be glad you did. I have invested MUCH time and effort to bring you what I hope is another <u>POWERFUL</u>, <u>AWE-INSPIRING</u> and <u>CAPTIVATING</u> book on NATURE.

In my first booklet, "The Unfathomable World of Things that Creepeth" (written over 20 years ago, and now in its second printing), I looked at the awesome world of beetles. It showcased the incredible design and complexity in one small portion of the animal kingdom that is often overlooked, ignored, or misunderstood.

In my second book, published in 2019, "High Tech vs The Highest Tech," I focused on examples of animals that demonstrate a technological nuance that defied the limits of man's capabilities: nano-design and complexity that cannot be explained by natural processes.

In this <u>NEW</u> book, "Nature's Believe it or Not," I have directed my attention to nature's odd-balls… the one-offs, the strange, and even extreme lifeforms. Those with outrageous design and seemingly impossible function that crush any naturalistic explanation.

In this book I will include PHOTOS that MEMORIALIZE PEOPLE and BLESSINGS throughout my life and ministry. My hope and prayer is that you will find TRUTH, LOVE, PEACE, and JOY in this life, and the life to come! It is written as a labor of love to my Lord and Savior, Jesus Christ.

May it be a blessing to you, my readers and friends,
-Jeff Tichelar

RECORD HOLDING TREES

First up: The Giant Redwood Tree

FACTS:

The TALLEST living thing in the World! (Not the oldest or largest –
but the TALLEST.)

Only two places in the United States where they grow:
* Pacific Coast in Northern California
* Southern Oregon near the ocean

Ninety-nine percent of coastal Redwood trees in the world live and
grow within the 40-mile long, Redwood National Park (the right eco-
system).

Many trees and plants only grow one place on the planet, which means they are "eco-system sensitive!" They must have just the right combination of temperature, rain, and fog. The Redwood trees need 85 to 100 inches of rain per year and a lot of fog. Along the coast where they grow, the water is cold. When warm air blows across this cold water, it produces fog. The sun then draws the fog into the coastlands.

August is a very hot, dry month with no rain. Only this fog keeps the trees growing and from losing their needles. The fog bathes the needles in moisture. That moisture drops from the needles to the ground and shallow roots, sustaining the tree until the rains come.

I know what you're thinking, you want to know how tall this tree is…

The tallest Redwood is over 375 feet tall, with many reaching 350 feet without breaking a sweat. Think of it – 350 feet, that's a 35-story high rise building (10 feet per story). Your ceiling height at home is commonly 8 feet. A 375-foot tree divided by 8 equals 47 rooms stacked up!

Their diameter averages 20 feet across with a 65 foot circumference. The roots are shallow, only 3-4 feet deep, but God knew what He was doing! They radiate out in all directions over 80 feet. This not only provides great strength and stability, but it also enables the tree to take advantage of the water that drips from the needles. Other trees that have deep roots would not survive in this eco-system.

The Redwood trees have bark that is 12-inches thick to protect them from fire, bugs, beetles, and woodpeckers. The bark has a water-based sap instead of oil based, so it does not burn easily. But I think the coolest trait our Lord decided to give this tree, was its SURVIVAL

SYSTEM. Only 10% of Redwoods grow from seeds. The rest come from sprouting out of the roots! There is a collar around the bottom of the tree with lots of sleeping buds. **If a tree is hurt or damaged, it sends a distress signal along with hormones to the buds.** The buds will sprout and start to grow in a ring around the tree using nutrients from the dying tree for sustenance. Often there will be as many as 100 new trees surrounding the old tree. The young trees grow quickly and within 20 years will often be 50 feet tall and about 8 inches in diameter.

Bristle Cone Pine

FACTS:

Record holder of OLDEST TREE – 4,828 years old! It is named Methuselah after the oldest man in the Bible.

The Bristle Cone Pine grows in the mountains of California. Methusaleh was the oldest known tree until 2013 when a second Bristle Cone Pine was determined to be even older at over 5,000 years old. The location and name have been kept secret in order to protect the tree from those who would do it harm. This tree was alive when Abraham was alive. WOW! That is fantastic!

Giant Sequoia

Facts:

Measurements: 280 feet tall with a 45 foot diameter, 102 foot circumference. (Estimated at least 3,500 years old.)

I would like to add one more record holder to this section on trees. The record of the <u>LARGEST LIVING THING</u> on earth: THE GIANT SEQUOIA TREE. These trees are named after an Indian chief! They are not the tallest, but the largest by volume. The most famous tree is named "General Sherman."

The volume of the trunk with no branches included is 52,500 cubic feet. This is equivalent to 30 average single family homes (17,000 square feet each), in other words, a city block of homes.

This tree would have been about 40-feet tall at the time of Moses. It only grows between an elevation of 5,000 feet and 7,800 feet. Its estimated weight is over 6,000 tons (12 million pounds). Think of the seed containing its DNA blueprint! The seeds take two years to grow inside a cone. Then it takes another 20 years before the cones open and let the seeds drop out.

What a picture of how God balances the reproduction of all life forms on earth. JUST RIGHT!

"The heavens declare the glory of God; the skies proclaim the work of His hands. Day after day they pour forth speech; night after night they display knowledge. They have no speech, they use no words; no sound is heard from them. Yet their voice goes out into all the earth, their words to the ends of the world..."
Psalm 19:1-4

• **NATURE** reveals the wisdom and power of God!

• Jesus uses **NATURE** to teach and communicate TRUTH!

• **All NATURE** (except some men) praises and acknowledges God's glory!

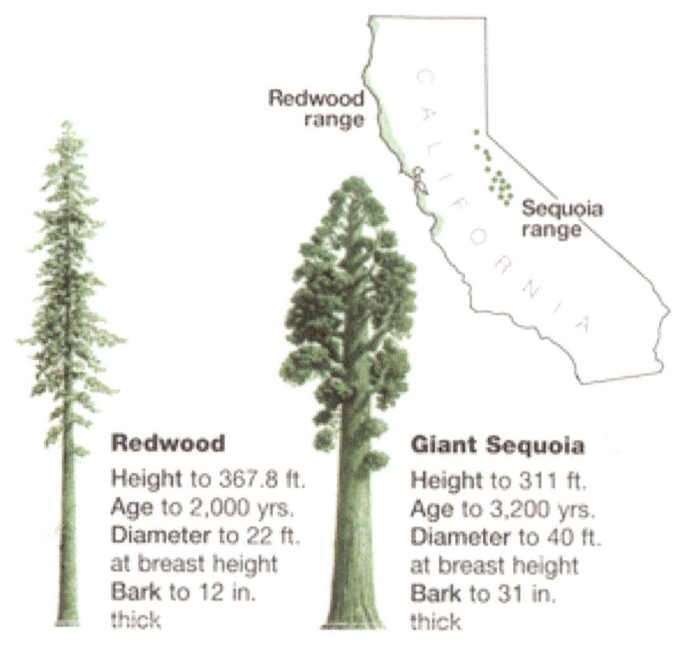

Redwood
Height to 367.8 ft.
Age to 2,000 yrs.
Diameter to 22 ft.
at breast height
Bark to 12 in.
thick

Giant Sequoia
Height to 311 ft.
Age to 3,200 yrs.
Diameter to 40 ft.
at breast height
Bark to 31 in.
thick

Giant Sequoias - World's Largest Trees

Space Shuttle   Redwood   Sequoia   Person   Blue Whale   Statue of Liberty   Brachiosaurus

Sequoia & Kings Canyon National Parks

THE LIMA BEAN STORY

We don't usually think of plants as being smart or taking an active role in their own defense... but we may have to reconsider that belief after looking at <u>our next creation</u>! THE LIMA BEAN – is all about self-defense!

It reminds me of the challenges of my own garden years ago. One common pest of many different plants is the spider mite. A primary enemy of the Lima Bean plant is the two-spotted spider mite. This mite injects its saliva into the plant's tissues, dissolving them. It just so happens that this mite has an enemy of its own – the <u>carnivorous mite</u>.

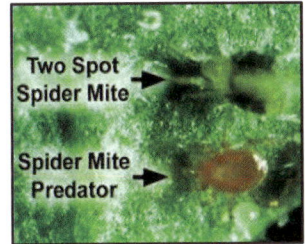

When attacked by the two-spotted spider mite, the Lima Bean plant sends out a special chemical distress signal. Neighboring Lima Bean plants receive the message and begin to send out signals of their own; even though they have not been attacked yet!

Are you kidding me? THIS IS AMAZING!

→ First - chemical messages are sent to different plants and plant "defenders."

→ Second - additional two-spotted spider mites are discouraged from coming.

→ Third - carnivorous mites, that are in the area receive the signal and come to feed on the <u>two-spotted spider mites</u>.

→ Fourth - Lima Bean plants have another enemy – caterpillars that eat their leaves… when necessary the Lima Bean plant can send out a **different** chemical message –"<u>calling in air-strikes by parasitic wasps</u>."

SO FAR (and this is not all) we have four different species receiving chemical messages!

1. Neighboring lima bean plants.
2. Warning to two-spotted spider mites.
3. Carnivorous mites to come fast.
4. Parasitic wasps to join the fight.

Please explain how this "extreme chemical (communication) warfare" could ever come about without a <u>MASTER CREATOR</u>. At this point I would like to quote from a very well-written research paper on Lima Beans. "Plant Whispers – Communication Skills of Lima Beans" Written by: Wilhelm Boland, November 9, 2015

> Plants communicate with their environment, especially by using fragrances. They converse with their peers and insects, and even other animals. They create different fragrances to chat with many different partners. A research team led by Wilhelm Boland at the Max Planck Institute for Chemical Ecology in Jena, [Germany]

examines the communication skills of the small lima bean. I visited him a few years ago."

He says that plants possess a large repertoire of different fragrances. "So far we know about a thousand fragrant compounds. There could be more." He sees my amazement and to put it into perspective adds: "Not all fragrances are present in one plant. Five to ten of these chemical fragrance compounds, however, are common to all plants. In addition, each plant can produce many different trace components."

Once a plant is under attack it sends out its first chemical message to warn other plants in the area! They too will respond by taking defensive measures of their own. What comes next is amazing. Continuing to quote from Wilhelm Boland's valuable research (book published 2015, "Plant Whispers – A Journey through New Realms of Science.")

"This response is only the first line of defense," he says, "more will follow immediately. After three to four hours, the Lima Bean produces a new fragrance bouquet to specifically attract beneficial insects to combat the bean's predators. So the bean calls in her bodyguards, so to say. **What is very interesting is how the Lima Bean can tell not only that she is getting hurt, but she also knows exactly who is hurting her."** When the lima bean is being infested by spider mites, she releases a special scent to attract predatory mites that feed on the spider mites. If caterpillars are attacking the lima bean, she sends out a slightly different fragrance to attract parasitic wasps that lay eggs inside the caterpillars. The eggs then hatch into wasp larvae and eat the caterpillars from within.

How can the Lima Bean tell if she is being attacked by a spider mite and not a caterpillar? She recognizes the saliva of the insect, says the researcher. "By now we know many of the chemical compounds of the insect saliva that enable the plant to determine exactly which enemy is attacking her." So the plant "tastes" the saliva of the predator eating away at her and then produces the fragrance that attracts the right "bodyguard."

What a great feat of communication! These types of symbiotic and cooperative relationships in nature scream of 'special creation'... while forcing evolutionists to say some really foolish things, i.e. "Oh well, if given enough time Genius, intelligence, and design will rise up from nothing."

Time does not answer the question of this level of complexity, the need for special information and communication. Here is a simple test, and feel free to take as much time as you like (weeks, months, years). Go into your backyard and from what you are able to take out of the ground, mix a chemical formula/potion that can summon any life form. You may protest that you never studied chemistry in school. Newsflash – neither did the plants, flowers or trees, and yet they can produce thousands of chemical fragrances that communicate and send specific messages to other plants and animals.

How can you deny that
INTELLIGENCE MUST COME FROM INTELLIGENCE?

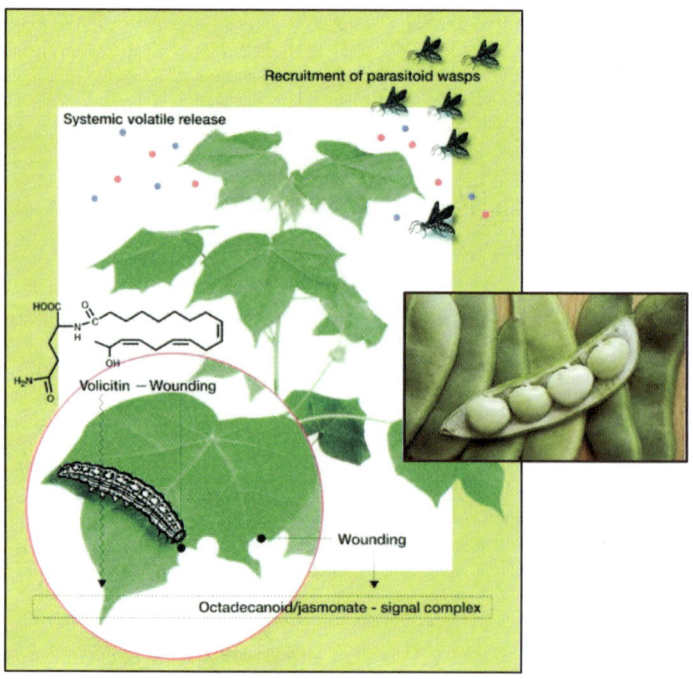

The Corpse Flower

These are real stinkers ☺

And now, our last two examples of similar, awesome plants. This will show you that we worship a GOD of variety and yes – One who has a sense of humor.

Facts:

The largest single flower on earth. The official name is RAFFLESIA, also known as "The Corpse Flower."

This unusual flower grows in the rain forests of Sumatra, Indonesia, and Malaysian Borneo. It can reach 36 inches – 3 feet across, and only blooms 6-7 days, every 4-5 years. But its real claim to fame is its fragrance! It stinks like a rotting carcass to attract its particular pollinators - carcass-eating insects.

Titan Arum Plant

Our second example of a really unusual and stinky plant – the World's Largest Unbranched Plant (flower) in the world. AMORPHO PHALLUS TTANUM shortened to "Titan Arum." This plant blooms every 7-10 years so it's a really big deal for plant lovers. I remember that on one of my visits to Sunrise Christian Academy, while driving I heard a news story excitedly talking about a botanical garden that had one of these "babies" on the verge of blooming! People were lining up to buy tickets days in advance. (My recommendation if you decide to go: eat light and bring a throw-up bag.)

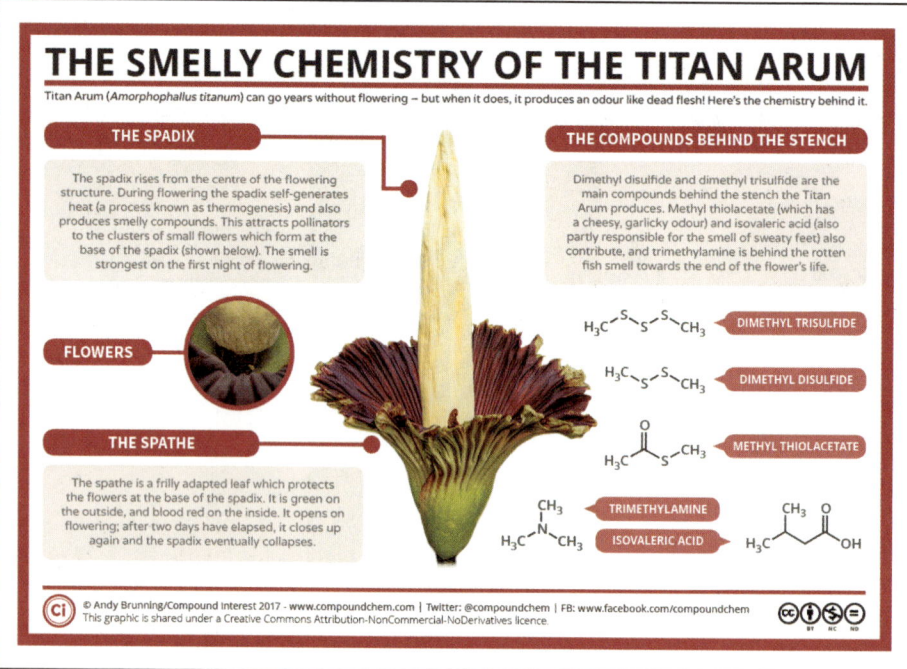

This particular plant can reach 10-feet in height. It has a dark burgundy color, combined with the smell of rotting meat to attract carrion (flesh) eating beetles and flesh flies for pollination. During the bloom, the tip of the SPADIX, reaches the approximate temperature of a human (about 98.6). Being ten feet tall causes heat (through the principle of convection) to rise up above the canopy and spread out like a "mushroom cloud." The insects follow.

The heat helps the "perfume" to VOLATILIZE and CONCENTRATE! The heat also helps with the illusion of a rotting carcass. Testing has revealed that this plant has it all when it comes to stench.

Chemical Analyses:

Dimethyl Trisulfide – limburger cheese
Trimethylamine – rotting fish
Isovaleric acid – sweaty socks

This would never evolve - never! The only thing this plant has in common with evolution is that when brought into the classroom both really <u>STINK</u>!

The fool says in his heart, "There is no God."
Psalm 14:1.

Madagascar Star Orchid
and Darwin's Hawk Moth

Here is an outrageous example of a mutual relationship between a plant and animal! The **Madagascar Star Orchid** is one powerful argument for SPECIAL CREATION!

It has an extremely long nectar tube... how long you might ask... it is 12 inches deep or 30 cm. In order to be pollenated, one of God's creatures will need to be equipped with a 12-13 inch "drilling rig," also known as tongue. That is one long tongue!

Keep in mind that God has created at least 15,000 species of butterflies and at least 150,000 different species of moths. NOT to mention thousands of other smaller pollinators like bees, etc.

Note: out of probably 250,000 (a quarter of a million!) insects, there is just <u>ONE</u>, one type of moth with the right equipment to pollinate the <u>Star Orchid</u>, with <u>NO backup</u>. (That is a God thing.)

It is nicknamed, "<u>Darwin's Hawk Moth</u>," scientific name Xanthopan Morgani. Darwin did not discover it, he merely took note of the orchid and concluded that there must be an animal to pollinate it. It was many years later the moth was discovered, proving there had to be a pollinator with special design! Another example of a "one-off" design by the Creator.

FULL DISCLOSURE - there is a debate over the moth's name... In the 1860's another evolutionary scientist worked with Charles Darwin; his name was <u>Russel Wallace</u>. They both marveled at what creature could possibly reach the plant's <u>syrupy treasure</u> buried <u>deep</u> in the nectar tube.

Some books and papers credit the discovery of the moth to Russel Wallace who referred to the moth as, Wallace's Sphinx Moth.

You can decide if you prefer to use the name <u>Darwin's Hawk Moth</u> or <u>Wallace's Sphinx Moth</u>. Here is my two cents: Man fights over who gets credit for the discovery of these marvels of nature, but I am more interested in the **ONE** who <u>designed and created</u> these marvels!

> "FOR SINCE THE CREATION OF THE WORLD GOD'S INVISIBLE QUALITIES—HIS ETERNAL POWER AND DIVINE NATURE—HAVE BEEN CLEARLY SEEN, BEING UNDERSTOOD FROM WHAT HAS BEEN MADE, SO THAT PEOPLE ARE WITHOUT EXCUSE"
> ROMANS 1:20

Albert Einstein (not a Christian) said the following in a concluding address to the faculty of the California Institute of Technology, **"Gentlemen, the deeper I delve into the sciences of this Universe, the more firmly do I believe that <u>ONE GOD</u>, or FORCE, or INFLUENCE has <u>ORGANIZED</u> all of it for our DISCOVERY."** He saw order and symmetry that he referred to as MATHEMATICAL ELEGANCE, but he could never comprehend that a God so great could also be our personal God…

Coelacanth
(pronounced SELA CANTH)

Coelacanth is believed to have evolved 340 million years ago and gone extinct about 70 million years ago. Fossils of coelacanth fish have been found in the same rock formations as dinosaurs.

Oh, oh, oh - in 1938, a rough year for the Darwin movement, scientists were informed that fishermen were catching coelacanth fish off the coast of Madagascar on a regular basis… good eatin' for a 340-million-year-old fish!

In addition, 10-20 years later, an Indonesian fisherman confirmed that they too had been selling (the living fossil) in the local fish market for years. The fact is that the evolutionist's promotion of "hundreds of millions of years to account for all the variety and complexity in nature" is just not true. That theory is based on endless assumptions and countless contradictions.

Staff at the National Museum of Kenya display a coelacanth fish caught by Kenyan fisherman in April 2001.

23

The great DIVERSITY of plant and animal life on this planet declares the glory and power of GOD! Important to note, coelacanth is not the only living fossil exposed. Others include corals, jelly fish, sponges, starfish, dragonflies, horseshoe crabs, millipedes, and more.

Evolution does not add up, God's perfect design does! Evolution requires change - a lot of change. That is why over the years as scientists have discovered and recognized greater examples of complexity and design in the animal kingdom, they are forced to provide some explanation. Thus, they have increased the estimated age of the earth by adding hundreds of millions of years with each new assessment.

The thing is, we do not see any examples of anything in nature evolving on a macro level. No evidence of new species forming. The opposite is true – rather than evolving, animals go extinct. Even more of a problem for evolutionists are the fossils labeled by Darwin as "Living Fossils." These are animals that were supposed to be extinct for millions of years only to be discovered alive and well in the 20th and 21st centuries.

- In Australia, there is a beetle that was discovered in 1998 that had been classified over 200 million years old.
- Dragonfly fossils that reveal a complex wing design and are virtually identical to dragonflies today, but the fossil has a classification of 300 million years old.
- Millipede fossils dated 430 million years old show no design change with those alive today.

One plant example would be the unique "Wollemi Pine," classified at least 150 million years old, but discovered in 1994-2000 west of Sidney, Australia. They are so protected that only a few researchers can get a permit to visit the forest for fear of contamination. Visitors must change into sterilized clothes to protect the trees from bacteria and viruses. They are worried about trees that are supposed to be 150 million years old.

You may find these additional nature facts about plants of interest.

Grass is a natural solar panel provided by an all-wise Creator to maintain balance in nature. Green growing grass captures sunlight and pulls CO_2 out of the air and sends it to its roots. If the grass is too tall or short it is not efficient. The cows that graze are the ones that prune and maintain the grass to just the right level which maintains an efficient CO_2 capture.

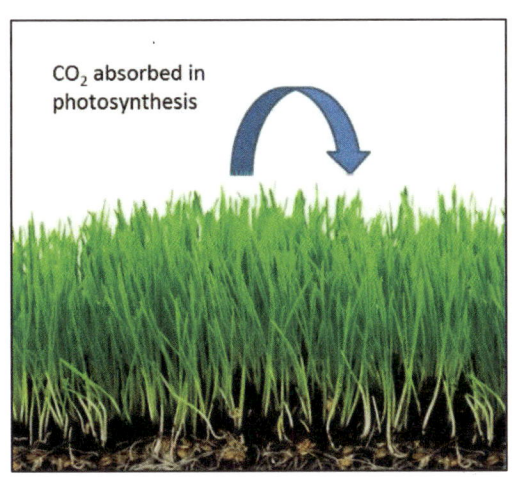

The forest in Guyana soaks up CO_2 at a massive rate (19.4 gigatons of CO_2 per year). The president of Guyana called out the hypocrisy of the West in March 2024 in a BBC interview by pointing out that the West has destroyed 65% of their forests while Guyana has maintained 95% of theirs. The truth is not always welcome, but available!

Cephalopods: Squid & Octopus

The cephalopod family includes squid, octopus, and cuttlefish. [For a study on cuttlefish see my book "High Tech vs. the Highest Tech" published in 2019.]

For our study we will highlight some strange and awe-inspiring features and behaviors of the squid and the octopus.

Squid

Cuttlefish

The **squid's head is triangular** shaped with its 8 arms in the rear. The **octopus's head is more round** in shape with its 8 arms more evenly distributed in a circle – like spokes on a wheel.

Octopus

The squid has 2 extra-long "feeding" tentacles (arms). The squid's tentacles are covered with specialized hooks and sucker rings with teeth. There are more than 500 species of squid ranging from 1-inch long full grown to giants reaching 60 feet in length! When feeding, the giant squid can shoot out its 2 "feeding" tentacles over 30 feet. They are tipped with hundreds of powerful sharp-toothed suckers.

The squid's 8 arms guide its meal to a sharp beak in the center of its arms. There the meal is sliced into bite-sized chunks. The chunks are then turned into ground meat by the "RADULA," a tongue-like organ in the squid's beak which is also covered with... you guessed it! More teeth!

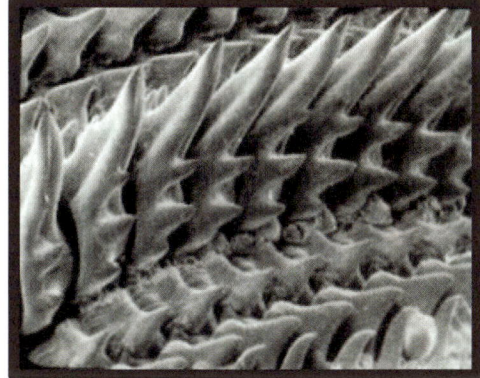 

The giant squid has eyes the size of dinner plates, one foot in diameter. Its complex brain is in the shape of a donut. The squid's esophagus runs through the hole in its brain. Bizarre YES, but it is a perfect, efficient, and unique design. The evolutionist is stuck with another example of a "one-off" design. There is nothing like it in nature to evolve from. Like a donut hole, the theory of evolution is hollow and empty.

One more amazing feature is that at the bottom of its body, there is an amazing multi-function tool called a FUNNEL. By pumping water and other fluids through its funnel, it is able to perform important tasks such as squirting ink, laying eggs, exhaling, expelling waste, and "booking out" by jet propulsion if needed for escape.

One species of squid (LOLIGO) is only 1-foot long and 3 inches wide, but its jet propulsion is awesome! It is so powerful; it has been observed by researchers and copied in water jets.

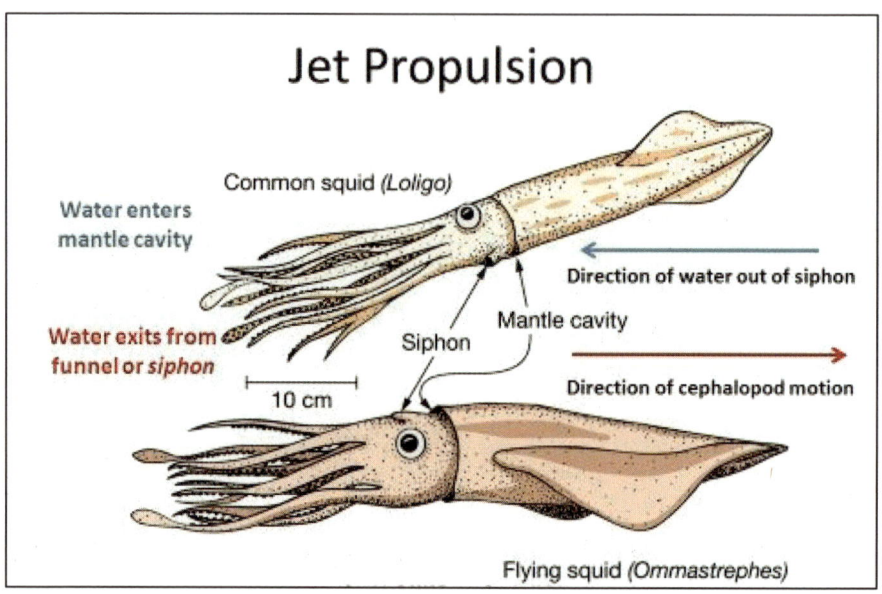

It can breech the water's surface up to 20 feet high and travel horizontally 150 feet. Its <u>mantle</u> is full of powerful muscles. Around the mantle is a "collar" that is open to receive water when jet propulsion is needed.

The brain then sends a signal to close the collar, and activate the insanely strong muscles in the mantle, producing an explosive blast of water thrust! **Try throwing a football from under water!** Water is also released just above the head through a special nozzle. The nozzle is multi-directional, controlled by both brain and muscles for fast and precise navigation. As the last drop of water is blasted out, the brain receives a message (in a fraction of a second) to open the collar, relax the muscles, and repeat the entire sequence IF necessary! Wow!

Now Meet the World's Best Mother...the OCTOPUS. So says science writer Jeremy Hance in the publication, "MONGA BAY-News and Inspiration from Nature's Front Line." July 30, 2014.

Scientists have discovered that the octopus has the longest brooding time of any animal on the planet. And yes, there are several other great examples such as the penguin and incubator bird. There are also good nurturing practices of both male and female animals throughout the animal kingdom... **BUT** I believe that after hearing the details of this mother, you will agree that she is in a class of her own.

In March 2007, marine biologists led by Bruce Robinson from Monterey Bay Aquarium Research Institute used a remote-controlled vehicle (RCV) to explore a deep-sea site in a canyon off of central California. At a depth of 4,583 feet, they noted a female octopus (Graneledone Boreopacifica) protecting its brood of eggs. [Common name: Giant Pacific Octopus.]

A month earlier this octopus was not at that location, so we have a pretty accurate starting point to observe something that had never been documented in the deepest regions of the ocean. Note: They have been observed in captivity and shallower water, but this was very different and unique! We now had an opportunity to document the length of brooding period of this **DEEP-SEA OCTOPUS**.

Fasten your seat belts!

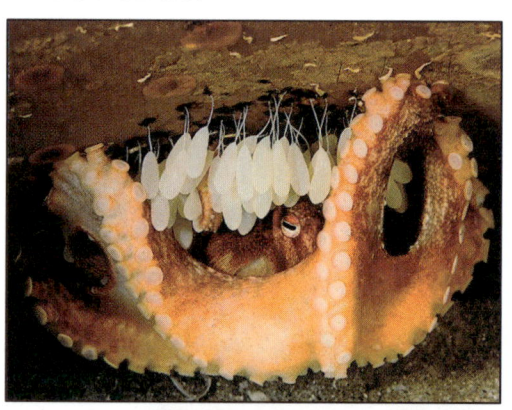

The scientists returned periodically to the site 18 times over a period of 53 months. That works out to **4½ years**!! Each time they returned they found the same octopus clinging to the rock ledge, arms curled around her eggs. The octopus was easily recognizable by scars from previous battles and the eggs were growing larger (confirming it was the same group of eggs.) You can actually see the babies growing inside the eggs in the bottom picture.

After 53 months in the autumn of 2011, the eggs hatched. On that last visit, the eggs were empty, and the mother was gone... (dead).

The late Paul Harvey always said, "Here is **the rest of the story.**" The rest of this story completely defies the main teaching of evolution – survival of the fittest, and the quest to survive.

It would appear that our Lord programmed this animal with a behavior that is something we cannot understand. The octopus's normal behavior is to give its life for her babies. This defies evolution because she is programmed **not to survive but to love**.

Here are some of the notes from those that observed this EPIC brooding period over 4 ½ years…

1. Although the mother occasionally shifted her position slightly, she always remained centered over her clutch of eggs. This is essential because the deep waters are full of predators that are desperate for a meal and the eggs would be a prized meal for sure.
2. The growing eggs need a constant influx of oxygen. The mother squirts water on the egg brood often to bathe them with oxygen.

I hope your seat belt is still fastened because the next fact is amazing!

3. While the mother cares for her babies she never leaves them. Not to eat - not for anything!
4. When the eggs are originally released from her body, they are in strands which are loose and floating freely. She must quickly gather them and braid them together by the thin cords hooked to each little tear-drop shaped egg. By the way, they are the size of a grain of rice!
5. She also manufactures a special underwater glue to fasten them to the roof of the ledge she has selected. The mother does not only refuse to leave for a quick meal, but when an easy meal happens by, she still refuses to eat. The food in the water could attract predators and the debris from eating could bring parasites to the eggs.
6. She only leaves once the eggs hatch, then she DIES, STARVING and EXHAUSTED!

As biologist Jim Cosgrove says, "No mother could give more."

The team that observed this mother over the 4 ½ years also noted that as the years passed, her condition deteriorated. Where she was originally <u>purple in color</u>, she turned <u>ghostly pale.</u> Her skin became slack, and her eyes became cloudy. She shrank in size while her <u>eggs grew bigger</u>.

As we consider this 53-month brooding period and try to make sense of it, I am encouraged in my conviction that only a great, loving and powerful Creator could program such a behavior into one of His creatures! **This would <u>NEVER EVOLVE</u>.** It is a wonderful example that God put in nature, examples of commitment, sacrifice and love.

Remember that our Lord displays the same commitment! He draws people to Himself with a promise that <u>whoever</u> comes to Him will be loved and forgiven of their sins. Jesus would ultimately seal that promise and commitment with <u>His sacrifice/His death</u> on the cross. Because of His great love for us! In the book of Hebrews (chapter 13), our Lord confirms His promise (to Christians) with the words, **"I will never leave you nor forsake you."**

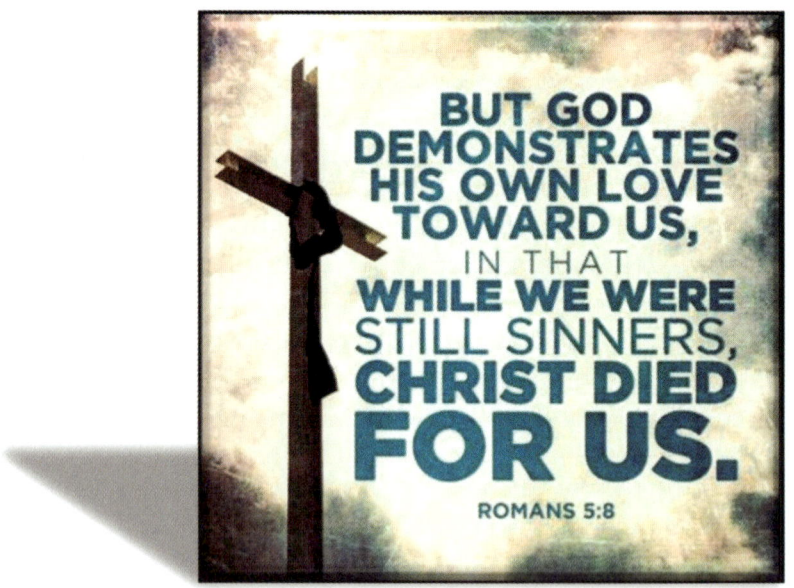

The Sea Cucumber

I call these the Kid's Favorite Creature (K.F.C.), both for the young and the young at heart! Sausage-shaped Sea Cucumbers gather food from the sea floor with sticky tentacles around their mouths. They are a plankton feeder, especially dead and decaying plankton.

Quoting THE SEA, "On muddy bottoms, (some) sea cucumbers push along, slowly scooping the organic slime into their mouths and licking their tentacle fingers like boys eating jam."

Their means of self-preservation is also unique. In a "Newsweek-Tech and Science" article by Kristin Hugo 10.12.2017, "Sea Cucumbers can puke up their guts (a tangled mass of internal organs) and grow new ones. Scientists are trying to figuring out how."

In case you are asking "Why?" It is because the entrails are left  behind to distract the enemy in order to get away. The lost organs will be replaced by the miracle of regeneration within a few weeks. They also have "great poop" which is in high demand to feed corals. The health of Coral Reefs depend on their poop.

I would love to have an evolutionist explain to me how the NEXT Sea Cucumber behavior developed. The behavior I am looking at is "slightly symbiotic (mutually beneficial)," though it only benefits one animal in this relationship. The sea cucumber has a very unique body design in which its respiratory system is connected to its rear-end/butt. That means the hole they breathe through is also their butt. The hole opens and closes like the aperture on a camera.

When the hole opens it attracts a certain type of fish called a Pearlfish. The Pearlfish loves to make its daytime home and resting area in the Sea Cucumber's rear-end. It feels so at home there that it will sometimes invite other Pearlfish friends to come in also. The Pearlfish slips out at night to feed and then returns.

**When I consider this animal creation, I am overwhelmed
by the variety, the unique design, and yes,
the sense of humor, of our Creator!**

Tardigrades

Tardigrade means "Slow Stepper" and is the name of a tiny (1mm) 8-legged creature discovered by a German pastor in 1773. They are also called <u>water bears</u> or <u>moss piglets</u>. There are more than 1,100 species of these free-living, tiny animals. They live everywhere and anywhere – preferring damp mossy areas, but can be found in <u>hot springs</u>, <u>fresh water</u>, <u>sand</u>, <u>ocean</u>, and <u>Antarctica</u>.

Most feed on algae, lichens, and moss, <u>piercing individual plant cells</u> with a special structure in their mouths, and sucking the cell dry. Some are also predatory carnivores. Pictures reveal their unique appearance, <u>face</u>, <u>mouth</u> and <u>claws</u>. But their greatest claim to fame is that they are <u>indestructible</u>!

- They can withstand temperatures of 150 degrees F. HOT!
- They can survive several hours of exposure to -458 degrees F! No other lifeform can survive that temperature!
- They can go 30 years without food or water.
- They are able to go into a death-like state called '<u>Cryptobiosis</u>' where they are curled into a dehydrated ball called a "Tun." It is also called a "<u>Tun State</u>" or suspended animation. This state allows them to survive extreme temperatures and long periods of time.
- Their eggs look like an alien spaceship.

- They can be found at a 20,000-foot altitude in the Himalayan Mountains.
- They are found at the bottom of the ocean in the Mariana Trench where the pressure is 1,000 times our atmosphere (that is 87,000 pounds per square inch.)
- They have survived pressure tests of 6,000 times earth's atmosphere which does not even exist anywhere on the planet.
- They can survive in a vacuum for 10 days with no oxygen including outside of a space shuttle.
- They can survive 1,000 times the lethal human dose of radiation and can self-repair their DNA if damaged.

Tardigrades are another example of amazing, unique design and function!

They are also another evolutionary headache, a "wrench in the theory." There is no animal that it evolved from. It is another "one off." In an article entitled, "How Long do Tardigrades Live?" by Emma Bryce, published June 2, 2018 she states that under normal circumstances the natural life span is thought to, "Rarely last longer than 2.5 years. But as stated, under extreme and deadly challenges – everything changes. When life becomes unbearable, these little wonders can go into survival mode... to the extreme!"

- By shutting down their metabolism
- By reducing their need for oxygen to near zero
- By emptying their cells of water
- By going into its "Tun" State (dehydrated ball)

In addition, they are also able to produce a special protein that protects its own cells. From a study in the Journal of Molecular Cells 2017, "It's thought that the tardigrade's talent for self-preservation comes down in part to its production of unique proteins that can lock fragile components into a position that protects the membranes, proteins and DNA from being shattered, pierced and torn when cells become desiccated (dried out)."

Is this evolution in reverse?
These are capabilities FAR beyond our own!

Meet "ONYCHOPHORA," The Velvet Worm

Here we go again... another example of the extremes some will go to, to explain away an animal that does not fit into their evolutionary framework.

Fossils of the Velvet Worm have been found in Canadian shale dating back to the Cambrian period. There is **nothing** in the animal kingdom that it could have evolved from and nothing that has evolved from it, frozen in time because the idea of special design by an all-powerful Creator is NOT an option for some people. Some scientific papers declare, "Unchanged from the time of dinosaurs – a living fossil." "Unchanged in 500 million years." Some have even suggested that it is a "missing link." But missing link between what animals? **The truth is... the Velvet Worm is a unique awe-inspiring animal and has its own identity!**

Onychophora, pronounced ony-chof-rans, means claw-bearer. This land-dwelling animal resembles a caterpillar in appearance, but that is where the similarities end. This animal is truly "one of a kind" in design and function! They are normally up to 4 inches long, but some grow up to 8 inches, with legs down the whole length of its body. Their skin is covered with a large number of papillae (small, round protuberances), forming delicate rows of overlapping scales that give it a velvety appearance.

The skin is "hydrophobic," meaning it repels water. The papillae each have a tiny hair at the tip that is sensitive to both touch and smell. Australian Velvet Worms have 14-16 pairs of stumpy legs. Some in other parts of the world have up to 43 pairs of legs. They have a smooth flowing movement when they travel, produced by an awesome and unique design.

There are no bones or skeletal system in this animal, including the legs. Movement is produced by a hydraulic (pressurized) fluid system. Awesome! They have 2 large antennae on their head, two oral tubes used to help capture prey, and two sickle-shaped jaws lined with teeth. They are also able to squirt a sticky slime from their oral tubes which is a cross between silly string and a glue gun. Once the sticky substance lands on its prey, it becomes rigid so the prey cannot escape. **It is a must** to pull up on YouTube a video of this animal using its "glue guns" to snare its prey… it is absolutely fabulous! What awesome design and function.

After the meal is snared (most often some kind of insect, beetles are a favorite), the Velvet Worm bites off various body parts and then injects digestive saliva into the prey to soften it up! Next, the insides are sucked up like pudding or a thick milk shake. Delicious!

In addition, each foot has a claw that is retractable. The Velvet Worm is able to detect prey through the touch and vibrations of their super sensitive sensing hairs. These hairs are so sensitive that the worm can monitor animal movements by sensing air currents.

Please notice the contradiction and/or confusion of thought concerning this animal. On one hand, said to be simple in design because it is from the time of dinosaurs. Its appearance is unchanged in fossils dating back to the Cambrian period. They call it primitive, one of the first signs of life – simple in design. **But what is simple in its design and function? Nothing!** Squirting glue guns, sensing hairs, hydraulic driven legs, our Lord has done it again… confounded those that refuse to accept a unique creation from an awesome Creator!!!

The Honey Badger

Pound for pound, the honey badger is the toughest, most determined, and most dangerous animal in the world. Just a little larger than a house cat, it is described by one researcher as being, "small, scrawny and they stink." Their name comes from their fondness for bee larvae, which makes them very destructive to unprotected bee farms.

Their personality and life code is well known and feared in the animal kingdom! They are described as tenacious, fearless, aggressive and highly intelligent. They are able to use and improvise a large number of tools including logs, branches, rocks, and other miscellaneous objects. One article gives this account, "A Honey Badger in a South African wildlife center escaped his enclosure twice to fight the lions in the exhibit next to his. He built towers out of rocks and sticks to climb over his wall and get to the lions. When they gave him a mate to be with, he stood on her head to unlock the gate and get out once again."

Honey Badgers never give up! If hungry enough, they will even swim underwater to catch a turtle or other aquatic animal to eat. (Not a normal diet or behavior.) Their normal diet is estimated to be about 25% snakes, including the most poisonous snakes. They survive the bites from venomous snakes and are able to tolerate hundreds of bee stings to get at bee larvae. Their ability to survive these poisonous snake bites is from an internal defense system that protects them from "alpha-neurotoxins that paralyze the muscles used in breathing."

It is not unusual to see a Honey Badger during a battle with a large snake receive a normally lethal bite or bites but keep fighting and kill the snake. They will then lay down nearby for a short nap while its body regroups, then wake up and eat the snake.

Their diet also includes just about everything including insects, birds, reptiles, bee larvae, small mammals, carrion (dead and putrefying flesh), fruits, baby crocodiles, rubbish, roots, and snakes. And they eat every part: hair, feathers, and bones.

Other interesting points:

- They have really thick skin, about ¼ inch, which is able to protect them from bee bites, and the arrows and spears of African bush hunters.
- Their teeth are razor sharp and they have mega-powerful jaws able to crack and chew bones and even turtle shells.
- They never back down even when confronted by much larger apex hunters like lions.

One last secret defense mechanism of the Honey Badger is that they have very loose skin covering their bodies. The honey badger is able to have great freedom of movement inside its strong, guardian coat of skin. Add to this a flexible spine and you have a secret "superpower!" **Large animals take a bite and think they have the little fella under control... Surprise!** The honey badger can completely twist and turn inside its skin into a position for a massive counterattack to the face of the attacker. With its over-sized claws and razor-sharp teeth, the attacker has no choice but to release the little fella.☺

Toughest Animal in the World

I am continually surprised and entertained by the countless examples in nature of incredible, unexpected design and complexity.

**But Who's design?
And what is the Source of complexity...
Intelligence?**

(Duck-Billed) Platypus

WOW! Here is another FABULOUS example of creative FLARE and LIMITLESS design. The question to be answered is **whose FLARE and LIMITLESS DESIGN**?

The Platypus is classified as a mammal because it has hair, breathes air, and nurses its young with milk. **But** it lays reptile-like eggs that are a half-inch in diameter, leathery, and soft. When the babies hatch, they are the size of a honeybee and blind for 11 weeks. They have teeth when young, but lose them as adults, replacing them with HORNY PLATES INSIDE their bill.

If all this is not strange enough, the mother has no mammary glands, the babies drink milk as it oozes from SPECIAL CRACKS in the mother's tummy. Adult males are approximately 20 inches long and weigh around four pounds. The females are smaller weighing two to three pounds. Platypus legs are short and thick.

The males have a VENOMOUS SPUR on their rear legs but are only VENOMOUS during the mating season of June through October. The venom is not fatal to humans but can cause a lot of pain.

The Platypus is found in fresh water in Tasmania, along the eastern coast of Australia and a few other remote locations. Some dishonest evolutionists in a desperate attempt to explain this odd animal tried to say that they are an example of evolution.

WHAT?
It is the opposite!
The Platypus is not just a wrench, but a whole set of
wrenches thrown into the evolution promotion machine!

There is NO animal that can be shown that the platypus evolved from and no animal that can be shown that descended from it. It is another of the countless "one-offs," in creation. It is an animal with no logical pre-platypus species or post-platypus species to point to. What we have is an animal designed to create wonder in children and adults alike. It is created to raise questions and promote discussion concerning the power, wisdom, and intelligence behind the design of such a diverse and complicated animal.

Something I've saved for last... its diet consists mainly of worms, insect larvae, and shrimp. So how does the platypus find food? Before I answer that question, it is important to enter certain facts into the record. When the platypus was first discovered some evolutionists were very quick to suggest that this was a "primitive," creature. Whatever that is supposed to mean. I would like to tell you directly that this animal is not "primitive." **The platypus has an incredibly complex electro-location system for finding food.**

The bill is covered with nerve receptors that can detect the ELECTRIC FIELD created when a shrimp moves its tail. The shrimp may be buried deep in the mud, but it cannot hide from a Platypus. Plus, the system must be super-efficient to meet dietary requirements. The platypus eats more than half its body weight in food every day!

Consider the wonderful description of the platypus High Tech Systems, quoting from, The Encyclopedia of the Animal World, 1972/vol. 15.

"The delicate skin covering the muzzle apparatus contains innumerable sensory organs innervated by branches of the trigeminal nerve which is absolutely and relatively enormous. The sense organs are tactile in function and since the eyes and ears are closed under water, the sense of touch in their muzzle is presumably the only means of locating food. Much mud and grit is ingested along with food and this doubtless helps in grinding up the crustaceans taken in. Platypus blood contains a lot of hemoglobin (up to 21g/100ml) and the oxygen capacity of the blood is high compared with that of other mammals. The high oxygen capacity of its blood enables the animal to maintain a large store of oxygen which helps in diving and staying under the water for long periods. The platypus can in fact stay under water for about nine minutes without harm."

Note how the article talked about the special design of the blood. So much for the so-called, "primitive" platypus with its highly oxygenated blood and its 40,000 super sensitive electro-receptors! The receptors on the platypus are able to detect the faintest electrical signals firing between the brain and tail muscles of a tiny shrimp buried in mud.

As we consider various examples of strange and complex animals, it is important to remember when debunking evolution, we must go to the beginning. It will not do to jump ahead to monkeys and other highly developed animals. We must start with lifeless matter and accept that there is no source of intelligence or the means to inject intelligence into an organism. They cannot account for the fact that there are no 2 or 3 celled animals. They cannot account for the reproductive capabilities in every life form. They have failed to construct a logical tree of life for all living things, **because there are no transitional fossils found – none!**

Evolution is a cruel life-affecting religion that leads its followers astray and away from the true Creator!

Locusts

The term "locust" is loosely applied to any large tropical or subtropical grasshopper. The term should be restricted to those that occasionally multiply into a great swarm and do catastrophic damage to vegetation. Africa suffers most from locust swarms.

There are three species: the red-legged locust, migratory locust, and desert locust. They exist in one of two phases, the solitary grasshopper or the gregarious (swarming) phase. When crowded together they change their behavior; and if kept like this for one generation or more, will change their shape and color.

Solitary When they first hatch, the solitary type disperse unless some odd environmental condition keeps them together. In the solitary phase they are usually green or brown to blend in with surroundings.

Gregarious (Phase Change) The gregarious phase is triggered by certain conditions like weather and favorable egg laying sites. Every female will lay 2-3 batches of 70-80 eggs. In this phase, the number after hatching, will multiply over 100 times. As crowding gets more intense, groups coalesce and move toward the phase change. Their color changes to a bold pattern of black and orange with yellow stripes. It wasn't until 1921 that scientists learned that the swarming and solitary locusts were the same insect.

I would like to share the well-written explanation for this mind-boggling transformation from, "Life Nature Library Series," vol. The Insects, 1962.

"It was found that the presence of mature male locusts, such as would be the case in crowded circumstances, makes female locusts mature rapidly. A chemical that the male secretes over its entire body stimulates the female's head glands, which release a hormone that speeds the maturation process. If female locusts are reared in the absence of males, many of their eggs fail to develop at all; those eggs that do, require about 28 days to mature. But when the females are reared together with mature males, their eggs grow to full size within 14 days or so.

This interaction between crowding and physical change in the female lies at the root of the mystery. All that is required to produce a swarm is a favorable season followed by an unfavorable one. In a favorable season, with abundant food, the population of solitary locusts will naturally increase. If the next season is a poor one, this increased population will be forced to crowd together in the few suitable areas that remain. The crowding exposes the females to male stimulus on a massive scale, females and their eggs mature at a headlong pace and a population explosion brings the locust horde into being.

As a swarm migrates in search of food and a place to lay eggs, the swarm grows at an unfathomable rate in the thousands and tons. The swarm may travel 1,000-3,000 miles. The plague will end normally due to weather conditions. The survivors will revert to the solitary phase."

According to, "The Animal Encyclopedia," if all the locusts in a swarm only 2 miles square were to breed successfully, in only 4-generations they would infest the entire 196 million square miles of the earth's surface!

Other Interesting Facts:
- Locust swarms, because of their dense concentration and size, often block the sun which cause darkness in the area.
- When swarms find an area with vegetation, they will eat every green thing and completely destroy the vegetation, plants, shrubs, bushes, trees…everything.
- Each locust eats its own weight in vegetation every day!
- Picture the size and impact of a typical swarm in East Africa – the wall of locusts was 100 feet tall and 1 mile wide. It was so long that it took 9 hours to pass moving at a speed of 6 miles per hour.

I'm reminded of a prophecy in the book of Joel in the Bible. God through His prophet wants to provide a picture of the future judgment and devastation that He has in store for the wicked. He describes a severe locust plague that hit Israel. In this he saw a sign for the final judgment and warns people "to repent." **The day of the Lord** will be a greater judgment yet in the future. Joel 2:2 says it is close at hand, "A day of darkness and gloom, a day of clouds and blackness…" Joel 2:11 says, "The day of the Lord is great; it is dreadful. Who can endure it?" What a plea to get right with our Creator!

The Blue-Footed Booby

There are six species of boobies, but no one knows the purpose of the blue boots. The Pacific coastline is the home of the booby bird along with many other water-loving birds.

These water birds have a variety of ways to grab a meal. Some are "skimmers" that fly over the surface of the water and snag fish swimming close to the top. "Shallow divers," as the description implies, are able to dive a few feet into the water. Then there are the "plunge divers" that can dive really deep.

The blue footed booby is a goofy looking bird that is fantastically designed, extremely successful at spotting fish, and able to time its dive attack perfectly. **Quick question... What would you consider to be a good dive for a bird?** 5 feet deep? 10 feet? 15 feet? 20-25? Remember we are talking about a bird. The Blue-Footed booby starts its dive from a height of 50 feet above the surface of the water, enters the water at a speed of 100 feet per second, roughly 70 mph and reaches a depth between 65 and 80 feet! It then grabs a meal and breaches the surface 20 seconds after entering the water. **This is awesome!** Please, if you don't believe in special creation, could you explain how such an awesome diving ability is possible? **Remember the booby is not guessing about maybe finding a meal down there.** No! From a height of 50 feet, the booby sees the fish, must calculate and adjust its dive to factor in the speed the fish is swimming, and at what depth. It must also allow for the refraction of water that distorts the actual location, and know how long it will take to reach the water surface plus the dive time through the water... and emerge with a mouthful! Wow!

The Geoduck

The geoduck, pronounced "gooey duck," is a very large saltwater clam. It makes for good eating. It has a shell approximately 6-8 inches long. Geoducks are commonly found on the west coast of North America. Its main claim to fame is its super long neck or siphon hose. The siphon hose (**Are you ready for this?**) can reach 36-40 inches. It is the largest burrowing clam in the world, and it has one of the longest life spans in the animal kingdom... up to 140 years! There is actually one that was documented to have lived 168 years.

It has various nicknames like mud duck, king clam, and elephant-trunk clam, for obvious reasons. Its burrow can be 3 feet deep in the sand, and it extends its siphon out at the surface. The Geoduck feeds by sucking water containing plankton through its siphon hose. After filtering the water, it ejects its waste through a separate hole in the siphon.

There are some record holders that have reached 15 pounds and measure over 6½ feet in length! And if you are wondering... that large, long, meaty siphon has a <u>savory flavor</u> and <u>crunchy texture</u>. In Korea it is eaten raw with spicy chili sauce. It is great in soups and stews.

I am continually struck by the fact that in nature, animals are more different than similar, which points to special design and creation!

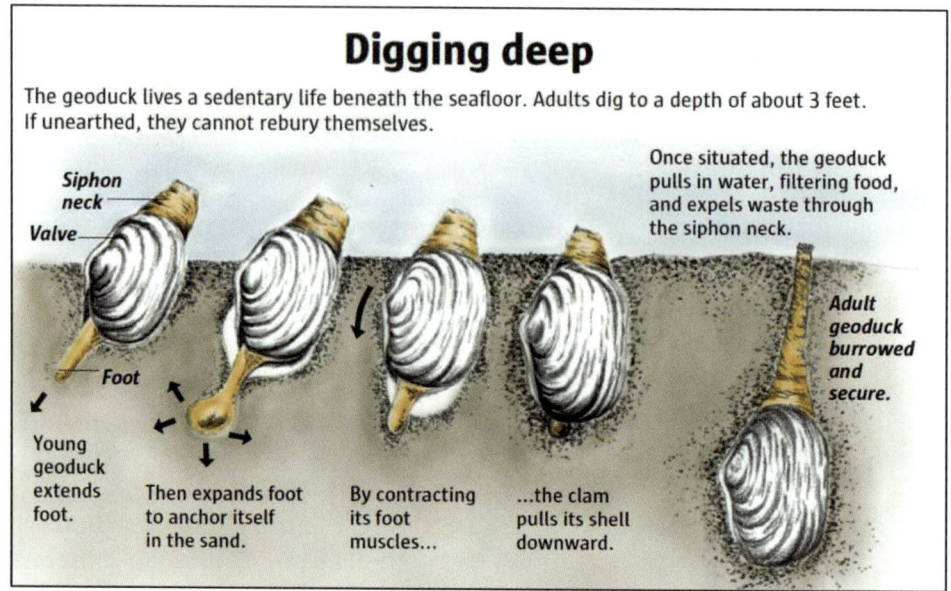

Digging deep

The geoduck lives a sedentary life beneath the seafloor. Adults dig to a depth of about 3 feet. If unearthed, they cannot rebury themselves.

Once situated, the geoduck pulls in water, filtering food, and expels waste through the siphon neck.

Siphon neck

Valve

Foot

Adult geoduck burrowed and secure.

Young geoduck extends foot.

Then expands foot to anchor itself in the sand.

By contracting its foot muscles...

...the clam pulls its shell downward.

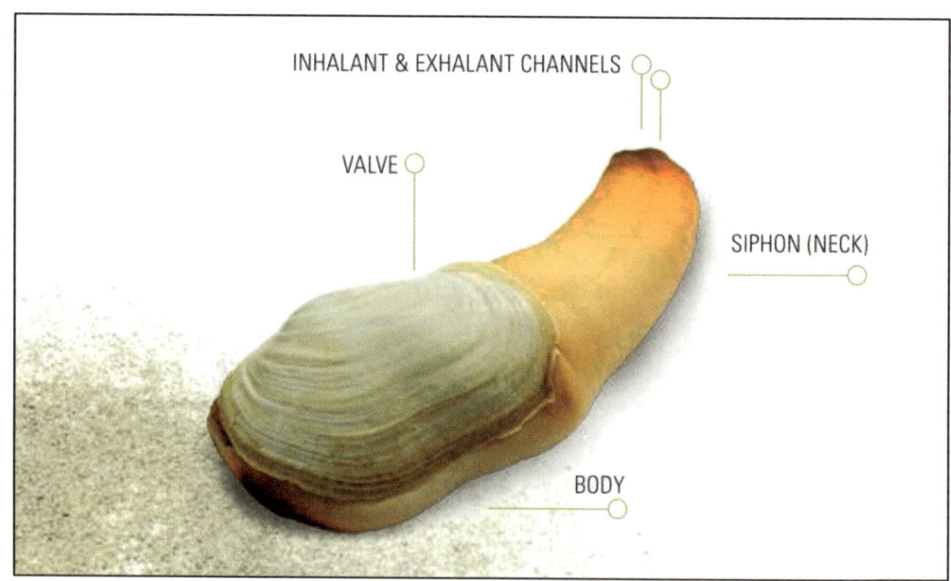

INHALANT & EXHALANT CHANNELS

VALVE

SIPHON (NECK)

BODY

The Dromedary Camel

The camel, also known as "the ship of the desert," is truly one of the most incredible animals on earth! The special design is on full display. Its home are the desserts of the Middle East. This amazingly engineered animal can eat almost anything, a piece of rope, leather sandal, material off a tent, a belt, old shoes, etc. Its mouth is tough enough to chomp on thorny cactus! Of course, its preference when available would be any kind of plant or grass that is common in the Arabian Desert.

Its single hump is packed with fat, not water! The fat is eighty pounds of life-giving body fuel. Food is often scarce in the desert, so this design is critical for survival and had to be in place from the start. It could NOT have evolved and survived!

Since water is scarce in the desert, when it is available the camel will take full advantage by downing 27 gallons in 10 minutes. What makes this possible is the incredible design God gave the camel. Blood vessels in the stomach absorb and transport the water throughout the body. In just minutes after drinking all that water, it travels throughout the body hydrating billions of special cells that are distributed throughout. Scientists have then tested the stomach 10 minutes after drinking 27 gallons of water and discovered that the stomach was already empty of all the water… **truly amazing!**

The camel gets its nickname "the ship of the desert" because it is so strong. It can carry a 400-pound load (the weight of many car engines) for a period of 8 hours with no break in the scorching desert. During those 8 hours, he can travel over 80 miles without eating or drinking.

It has been documented that in some extreme cases, a Dromedary Camel went 8 days without a drink. During that extreme example the camel lost 227 pounds off of its normal weight of 1,000-1,100 pounds.

The camel will look skinny with its ribs showing because all those billions of cells have lost their water reserves. If necessary, the camel can pull water from its blood. Normal blood is 94% water, but by design the camel can give up 40% of the water in its blood and still be healthy. **Such an example of extreme design to survive in the hot, dry desert is remarkable!**

Consider the fact that if we as humans lose just 5% of the water in our blood, we go blind. If we lose 10%, we will lose our hearing and not be able to function. At a 12% loss of water, the blood thickens, and we DIE! Our blood cells are round, but the blood cells of the camel are elongated, which is different by God's design. This allows their blood to circulate effectively even when the camel is severely dehydrated.

Next, have you ever tried walking in sand? (At the beach, etc.?) It is not easy and requires a lot more energy. The camel has specially designed feet. His hooves are wide and become even wider when walking, with a bit of extra skin between his toes like webbed feet. They don't sink into the sand. **With this awesome design, the camel can travel at 10 miles per hour.**

Sandstorms are common in the desert so more special design is needed. They have muscles in the nose to close the openings and keep sand out but leave just enough air coming in to breathe. The eyelids arch over the eyes like screens blocking sand and sun while maintaining vision. If a grain of sand gets past the defenses, there is an inner eyelid that automatically wipes the sand off the eyeball like a windshield wiper. **I believe this is a clear example of special design for a specific environment.** There is no time for transition and for these unique designs to evolve. The camel could not survive in the desert without its special design and amazing equipment being in place from the beginning!

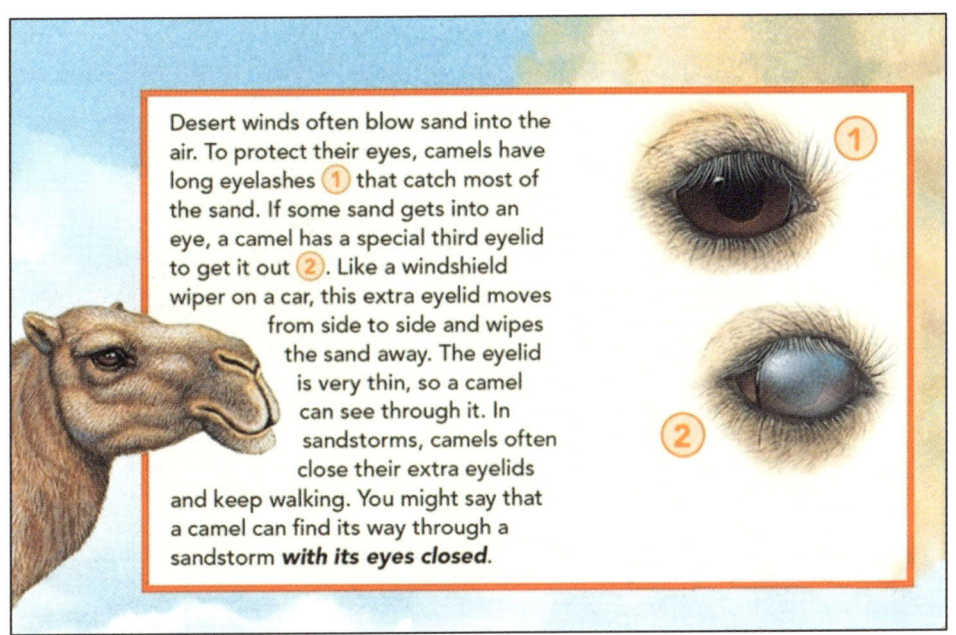

Desert winds often blow sand into the air. To protect their eyes, camels have long eyelashes ① that catch most of the sand. If some sand gets into an eye, a camel has a special third eyelid to get it out ②. Like a windshield wiper on a car, this extra eyelid moves from side to side and wipes the sand away. The eyelid is very thin, so a camel can see through it. In sandstorms, camels often close their extra eyelids and keep walking. You might say that a camel can find its way through a sandstorm **with its eyes closed**.

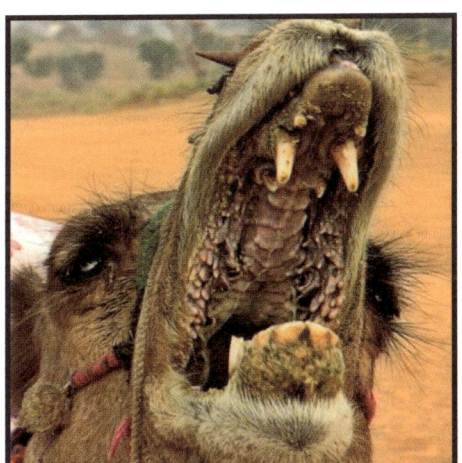

Warning: the next three animal examples and lessons are based partly on biblical insights and information. No offense is intended if you have different beliefs, but I think you will be amazed.

The Piddock Clam

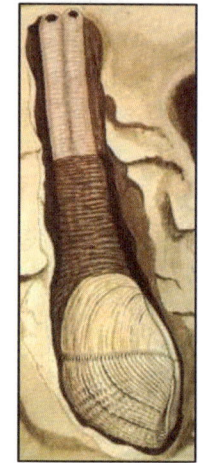

Piddock clams are in the mollusk family. Sometimes they are referred to as "boring clams" and "angel wings," which describes the shape of their shell. They begin their lives as free-swimming larvae. At this stage of their lives, they belong to the group of organisms known as zooplankton. In the transformation from a little worm-like creature to its adult form there is a release of a special liquid from the larvae's skin. That skin layer is also referred to as the mantle, as the liquid hardens it forms the shell.

The clams need to find the right kind of stone for the next stage of their lives. Once the Piddock grows a shell it begins to drill a burrow. Their choice of locations is in shale, chert, or soft siltstone. They arrive at adulthood in 3 years and can live for 20 years and reach 6 inches in length.

This clam lines its burrow with a protective layer of calcium carbonate. This layer is protective and seals the Piddock into its home permanently. One of the most important features of the piddock is its dual siphons. A larger siphon tube that is fringed with filters for collecting food and a smaller siphon tube used to get rid of waste. The siphon tubes are also used to pump water in and out of the shell. The water pumped in is passed over highly vascularized gills designed to absorb oxygen.

Formed in two halves, also called valves, and held together with a hinge, the shell grows as the clam grows. Programmed into its behavior as the shell is formed is the desire to attach itself to an ocean rock and to start to drill. Now consider the details of this life cycle... As the mature Piddock bores into the rock for safety deeper and deeper, it will never be able to leave its rock home. The siphon tube pump system is the only system that provides this protected clam a means to feed, expel waste, and supply oxygen. **How could such a strange, unnatural, and complicated system ever evolve? It didn't!**

As the clam grows, it must continue to bore deeper into the rock increasing the size of the hole cavity as it goes deeper in, but smaller behind. How? Sharp edges on the front edge of the shell rasp into the rock with a back-and-forth movement. This movement is not normal behavior for a clam. This is the only clam that behaves this way; the only one that moves forward but can't reverse.

Another outrageous design feature involves **five special glands** to aid in feedings. When hungry, the clam is able to release a green mucus from these glands through its siphon tube into the water. It does this in a dark environment which attracts many small sea creatures like plankton. How does the plankton find the green mucus in the dark? I forgot to mention the green mucus is a bright, luminescent light. It glows in the dark! Once the food has been drawn to the green luminescent mucus, the clam turns its suction on and food is sucked down the tunnel in time for dinner.

This clam can teach several spiritual lessons! Safety in the rock is a typecast in the Bible. Psalm 18:2 says, *"The LORD is my rock, my fortress and my deliverer; my God is my rock, in whom I take refuge, my shield and the horn of my salvation, my stronghold."* It tells of Jesus being our rock, and if we belong to Jesus, we are safe in Him just as the clam is safe in the rock. When we know Jesus, we should always be growing and digging deeper into our relationship with Him. There should never be a thought to go back to a life without Him. He is our source of life and safety. This we achieve not by boring into the rock but by having faith in our Rock!

Coccus Ilicis – The Scarlet/Crimson Worm

The unusual and biblically significant life cycle of the Crimson Worm is truly of epoch importance. In ancient times the Crimson grub or Scarlet Worm was very rare. The dye produced was the color required by the high priests of Israel for their temple garments. Thousands of crushed bodies were required to produce the deep, beautiful crimson red color. The dye never faded! And could never be washed out.

The worm, when preparing to give birth, climbs the tree (the Kermes Oak) of its own choice, knowing that it will die there. She goes to the tree to give birth and life to her children. She lays her eggs on the tree and then attaches her body over the eggs. During the process she secretes a crimson fluid that covers her body and the eggs, and it stains the tree. The stain will never fade from the tree.

Note: During the process she permanently impales herself to the tree over the eggs. Psalm 22:6 written 1,000 years before the birth of Jesus, prophecies the words of Jesus. "But I am a <u>worm</u>, and not a man, a reproach of men and despised by people." The word "worm" in Hebrew is "towla," which means crimson. The verse is saying, "But I am crimson," referring to the blood that Jesus would shed for us on the cross. What a prophecy! And it was made 1,000 years before Jesus's birth!

Notice the parallels. Like Jesus, the Crimson Worm goes up the tree voluntarily for the salvation of her children. Just as the crimson fluid that is released marks the mother's body, eggs, and stains the tree, Jesus's blood marks those that come to Him for eternity. The blood will never lose its power!

The worm is also used to make heart medicine. On the tree, it releases an anti-bacterial agent to protect the eggs. The Bible says that the blood of Jesus cleanses us from all our sins. Isaiah 1:18 says, *"Come now, and let us reason together, says the Lord, though your sins are like scarlet, they shall be as white as snow; though they are red like crimson, they shall be as wool."*

After dying, something amazing happens to the Crimson/Scarlet Worm. For 3 days, the worm appears as described, a worm protecting her eggs. But on the 4th day, the worm has curled up, pulling its head and tail together in the shape of a heart. And though the tree and babies are permanently stained, a wax-like material forms on the worm's body which is white as snow. Yes, white as snow and wool, a picture of the power and result of Jesus' blood washing away our sins… His blood is the payment for our salvation!

There are whispers of Jesus throughout creation!

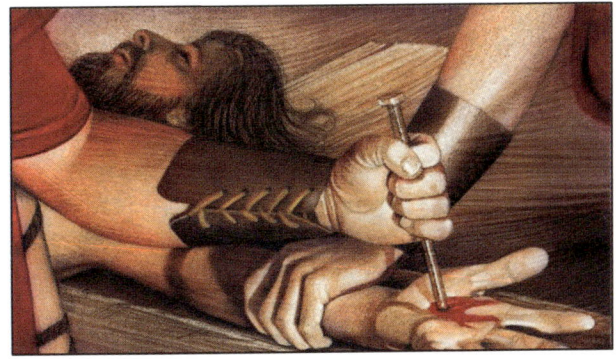

The Lamb

The lamb is <u>unique</u> in all God's creation! In the Bible, several animal sacrifices are associated with different aspects of Jesus's life and death. The dove speaks of purity and gentleness. The ram and the bull speak of power and strength. There is one that clearly stands out from the rest and has been used more in scripture to picture Jesus than any of the others …the Lamb! Jesus is given a very prominent name in scripture, **"The Lamb of God."** When Jesus began His earthly ministry and John the Baptist saw Him approach, he declared in John 1:29, "Behold the Lamb of God that takes away the sin of the world."

The apostle John, in a vision recorded in the Book of Revelation, speaks of seeing, "A Lamb, looking as if it had been slain, standing in the center of the throne," and those in heaven falling down before "the Lamb." (Revelation 5:8) Looking slain is a reference to Jesus's death on the cross. Standing in the throne room points to the resurrection and the Lord having conquered sin and death. Revelation 12:11 declares that we can overcome Satan by the blood of the Lamb. Jesus said, "I am the Good Shepherd." (John 10:11)

Keep these thoughts in mind as we consider the lamb more closely. **Both the lamb and the shepherd become powerful pictures or types in the Bible.**

- No other animal or class of livestock requires as much care and attention!
- The lamb is the only animal in God's creation with no natural defenses.
- **It is the only animal <u>unable</u> to survive without a shepherd.**
- Sheep and especially lambs lack <u>good sense</u>. When thirsty for example, they become restless and will drink from any source of water if not led to clean water. That is a huge problem because their immune system is similar to our own (unlike other animals) and will become deathly sick from polluted water. They can pick up internal parasites like nematodes, liver flukes, and other germs and disease.
- Sheep and lambs are thin skinned, contrasted with wolves, deer, and other animals that thrive in cold weather. If a lamb gets wet and then chilled they are susceptible to colds and pneumonia and even death.
- Without being led to green pastures they will gnaw at the same barren pasture relentlessly and drink water from a mud hole.
- And even if they lie down, unless they are free of fear, they will often become anxious and disoriented from a lack of rest.
- As a sheep or lamb grazes (without defenses) it is easy prey for cougars, lions, tigers, coyote, etc.
- One of the more pathetic sights and reasons a shepherd must search hard for a lost sheep or lamb is their poor sense of direction. They will get lost a few miles from their home. Think of the contrast with migrating birds and other animals who have a keen sense of navigation.
- Sometimes when exhausted a sheep will lie down with legs folded underneath. But if it rolls over and has a heavy fleece, it may roll over too far onto its back and its feet go up in the air. Bleating for help, it becomes panicked, fearful, and thrashes around in frustration. If not found soon it will be easy prey for buzzards, vultures, and coyotes. (The position is called a "cast.") As it struggles in this position, gases build up in the rumen, blood circulation is cut off to vital organs and to its legs and it can die

in hours. In the "cast" position, sheep will die 100% of the time if not found by the shepherd!

As you consider the life of a sheep or lamb and the fact that they must have a shepherd, do you **see any problem for the theory that they evolved**?

The Bible says Christians are the sheep and Jesus offers to be our shepherd, our "Good Shepherd." Consider the plight of a lamb without a shepherd? Consider our plight without Jesus! By design, man is created to thrive in fellowship with God. Without that relationship we are like the lamb without a shepherd. We miss out on providential protection, having a source of wisdom and direction, warning and instruction from His word, peace, love, and joy on the highest level, and the promise of an eternal home which is our heavenly hope.

Psalm 23:1-2

The Lord is my shepherd; I shall not want.

He maketh me to lie down in green pastures:
He leadeth me beside the still waters.

Baby's First Language

- There are approximately 7097 languages worldwide.
- This amount fluctuates, but there are at least 7000 at any given time.
- Language and communication are as vital as food and water.
- We communicate to exchange information and build relationships.
- Language is a very important tool for exchanging emotions, feelings and ideas.
- The phrase "mother language," refers to what we are taught at home from birth by our parents. The mother language is the core of a person's culture.

A Challenge to Parents

Would it surprise you to know that the first language of every baby in the whole world is the same? That is because a baby's first language is creation! Animals, plants, smells, colors, touch, taste, feel… It doesn't matter where you are from or what you believe – the first year is spent experiencing God's awesome creation. How exciting it is to see everything through a baby's eyes! **Creation is every human being's mother tongue from birth.**

Creation is the core of a Christian's culture. So, the mother's language is the core of a person's culture. Creation, our mother tongue, is the core of our culture as Christian's. And every human being has the chance to claim it as such! Psalm 19:1-3, says "The heavens declare the glory of God; and the firmament showeth His handiwork. Day unto day utters **His speech**, and night unto night shows His knowledge. There is no speech nor language, where His voice (the voice of creation) is not heard!" Creation is God's voice!

God speaks to us and our little babies through His awesome creation. Then what happens after this great start? Tests have been performed on children who are adopted from one country and brought to another. Almost without exception, within a short time, the child has no memory of its first language – it is lost to the new country and new language. AND in most places around the world, the mother tongue of creation is also drowned out by worldly systems and other religions.

The only exception is if the child had someone in his life that spoke his mother tongue. **God will always be in our lives speaking our mother tongue to us.** There will never be a time in any person's life where God is not crying out and communicating to mankind **individually** through His creation. "There is no speech nor language, where His voice is not heard!"

The question is… are we listening?

In a world that throws many ungodly "languages" at our children, it is our responsibility to help preserve their mother tongue. You may not think just one book that says dinosaurs roamed the earth millions of years ago or a few lessons on evolution will hurt. The Bible teaches that dinosaurs and man walked together in a recent creation. You might think that one cartoon series about vampires, zombies or witches is okay, but unwittingly, you are allowing that content to destroy your child's mother language. And I promise you, there will be consequences as they get older.

You may say this is too strong a message, but one child, especially one with parents who seek to follow the Lord, can affect many! The Bible is always giving an example of the power of one – one person with convictions and courage. Yes! It must be a strong message!

-Cynthia Kocher 2020, a wonderful devotional
by a dear sister and blessing in my life.

Evolution's "Tree of Life"

One of my goals in writing this book was to show the evolutionist's impossible attempt to put all life forms in an <u>orderly</u> and <u>complete</u> "Tree of Life," story and illustration. **The variety, complexity, and diversity of function SCREAM special design!** The countless unique "<u>one-off</u>" plants and animals and so-called "<u>living fossils</u>" reveal the foolishness of this evolutionary belief.

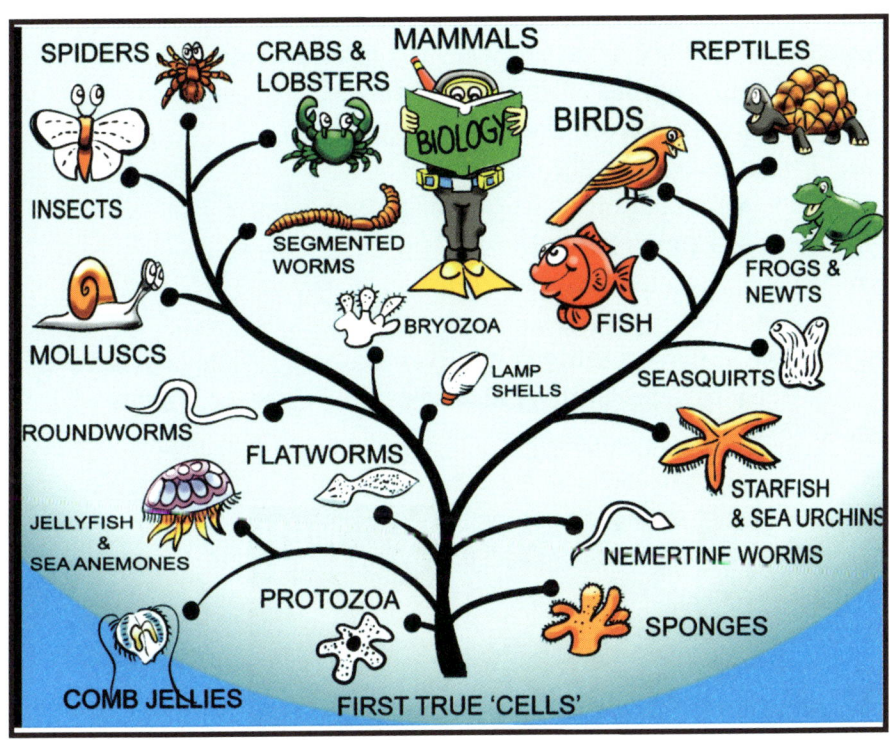

Remember that the "theory of evolution" is based on the idea of small changes over long periods of time to produce the magnificent plants and animals that fill our planet. Instead, what we discover is an endless number of ultra-complex plants and animals, species that differ in every possible way, life function, defense, feeding, reproduction, etc. The differences we see are not "small changes," but are often unexpected, odd, strange, unique, AND even awe-inspiring. **Every one of them is a masterpiece of complexity and function!**

There is nothing like it before or after. The imagined theory of evolution provides no branches for a "Tree of Life." What we find in nature is Intelligent Design, not disorder or random natural processes. **Important to note…** This is also what we find in the fossil record. All the "so-called" missing links are still missing. There is <u>NO</u> evidence or record of any life form changing into a different life form. All fossils are fully formed and functioning life forms. And remember we have billions of fossils today to examine. If evolution happened, we would see the (hard) evidence!

There are at least six miracles every evolutionist (atheist) must believe:
1. Existence comes from non-existence.
2. Order comes from chaos.
3. Life comes from non-life.
4. The personal comes from non-personal.
5. Reason comes from non-reason.
6. Morality comes from matter.

In other words, everything came from nothing. "The fool says in his heart, there is no God." Quote from our Creator, Psalm 14:1.

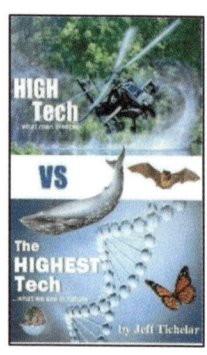 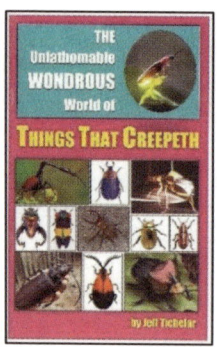 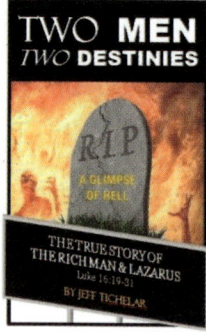 Other books/booklets by Jeff Tichelar available through our website (listed below) and our ETSY store.

If you liked this book, you will find similar stories in my book, **High Tech vs The Highest Tech**, and in my booklet, **The Unfathomable Wondrous World of Things That Creepeth** and a completely different story in **Two Men Two Destinies (A Glimpse of Hell).** Go to: www.bibletipnow.org.

Follow the Science!

Probability is a numerical value given to show how likely or not something could happen. The numbers or odds are calculated by mathematics and are ESTABLISHED SCIENCE. When we look at the complexity of life through the Laws of Probability, the numbers are breathtaking!

Note: an important reference to understand is the size of numbers we are talking about. Consider the number of atoms in the observable universe, 10^{78}-10^{82}.

That is 10 followed by 78 zeros
(10,000,000,000,000,000,000,000,000,000,000,000,000,
000,000,000,000,000,000,000,000,000,000,000,000,000,000)
to 10 followed by 82 zeros!
(100,000,000,000,000,000,000,000,000,000,000,000,000,000,000,000,
000,000,000,000,000,000,000,000,000,000,000,000,000)

The numbers are mindboggling!

Before we ever get to the probability of 1 living cell coming into existence by natural processes, we must look at what makes a cell. We need **amino acids** to get **proteins** and **protein** to get **DNA** (the blueprint of life). That is a BIG problem to overcome right from the start for those that believe in natural processes. There can be NO protein without the exact correct sequencing of amino acids. (That is a separate study for those that would like to investigate it.) And we cannot get protein without DNA. There is no natural explanation for life. There is only **supernatural** direction from outside the process!

Now, setting aside the need for supernatural intervention right from the start, and looking at the numbers/odds of life systems coming into existence by themselves, **we are blown away!**

There are approximately 375 amino acids in a medium size protein. Some bacteria have approximately 267 amino acids. Now consider the odds of one <u>simple</u> protein containing just 150 amino acids forming by chance. That number is 10^{164th} power! **That number is twice the number of atoms in our universe!** Professor Rick Ramashing (an Agnostic) and Sir Fred Hoyle set the probability of a cell forming by chance at $10^{40,000th}$ power! Can you imagine a 10 with 40,000 zeros? Carl Sagan estimated the chances of a man evolving at $10^{2,000,000,000th}$ power (that is 10 with 2 billion zeros!)

Honest scientists of all beliefs consider any number over 10^{50} to be impossible. The laws of probability in SCIENCE set the limit of possible to impossible at 10^{50}. Unfortunately for many Evolutionists, Agnostics and Atheists in the scientific world, it is not a matter of science but of faith. Against IMPOSSIBLE ODDS, some choose to believe a LIE.

PLEASE FOLLOW THE SCIENCE!

Your current wellbeing and future eternal life both depend on your heart and mind being open to hear and receive the TRUTH.

A heart felt message from the author...

Thank you for taking the time to read this book. I pray that you would understand the clear implication of God's incredible design in nature. Pause for a moment and consider the tremendous effort and complexity God has woven into nature in order to capture the attention of the youngest child and the most accomplished scientist. Jesus is constantly, lovingly, seeking to get our attention, so that we would receive His message of love, and understand our need for salvation. Once He has our attention, we must respond to His plan for salvation.

Two common attitudes that keep people from salvation are:
1. I'm okay, I'm not that bad, God will accept me as I am.
2. God will not send a "basically good" person to hell - the old argument that a loving and merciful God will not send sincere, well-meaning sinners to hell.

My friend, if you could live a life worthy of heaven (perfect), then Christ would have died for nothing. No person can be forgiven apart from Jesus Christ!

"As it is written: There is no one righteous, not even one; there is no one who understands; no one who seeks God. All have turned away, they have together become worthless; there is no one who does good, not even one."

"Therefore no one will be declared righteous in God's sight by the works of the law; rather, through the law we become conscious of our sin."
-Romans 3:10-12, 20 NIV

For it is by grace you have been saved, through faith—and this is not from yourselves, it is the gift of God - not by works, so that no one can boast.
-Ephesians 2:8-9 NIV

If you believe that the love and mercy of God will insulate you from the penalty of hell, consider this, "Where was the love and mercy of God when His only Son was being brutally crucified?"

This question is difficult to answer because you do not comprehend the seriousness of your sin, and the unfathomable depth of God's love. In order to remain righteous - God must judge sin! In order for God to demonstrate His love, He must act! And act He did! God's solution was a substitutionary death. In other words, He paid our sin debt Himself. That is why trusting in Jesus is not optional, it is the only solution to our dilemma.

Expecting to enter heaven, without trusting that Jesus died on the cross in our place is like saying, "I believe Jesus died on the cross, but He did not have to die for me. I'm okay, I'm not that bad, God knows me..." Yes, God knows we are self-deluded, prideful sinners that are more interested in doing things our way than submitting to His Word. God tells us that we must accept Jesus as our Lord and Savior!

Salvation is as simple as ABC:

Agree with God that we are hell deserving sinners and turn from sin.

Believe that only trusting in the finished work of Jesus and asking Him to be **YOUR personal Savior** is the answer.

Confess your decision for Christ with others as you live for Him and Praise His Name!

You have the God-given freedom to think and believe whatever you choose but remember, all our choices have consequences! So before you make a choice concerning something so important – at least take the time to consider, just a little of the evidence for creation. The wonder of "Intelligent Design" has successfully been blocked from entering many of the classrooms in America, where only ideas that support the accepted or official theory are allowed. I hope I have remedied that in this book, and you now realize how much God loves His creation and how much He loves you!

Jeff's Favorite Creation Verses ∽

Psalm 104:24 (NLT) - "O Lord, what a variety of things You have made! In wisdom You made them all. The Earth is full of Your creatures."

Psalm 33:8 (KJV) - "Let all the earth fear the LORD: Let all the inhabitants of the world stand in awe of Him."

Job 12:7-10 (NIV) - "But ask the animals, and they will teach you, or the birds of the air, and they will tell you; or speak to the earth, and it will teach you, or let the fish of the sea inform you. Which of all these does not know that the hand of the Lord has done this? In His hand is the life of every creature and the breath of all mankind."

Jeff's Personal Salvation Verse ∽

John 11:25 (NIV) - "...I am the Resurrection and the Life. He who believes in Me will live, even though he dies..."

Jeff's Life Verse ∽

Romans 1:16 (NKJV) - "For I am not ashamed of the Gospel of Christ, for it is the power of God to salvation for everyone who believes…"

About the Author…

Jeff & Team in Quito, Ecuador 2001
Building and Medical Mission Trip

"Riverdale Fellowship" - an outreach ministry founded at the
Riverdale Marina, by Jeff and other Christian brothers in 2005

Three-man team built home for the missionaries in the Amazon
Jungle in 2001. Jeff with children from the Satta Maui Tribe.

Jeff in the Amazon Jungle with the Mission Team. Building
a four room school house for Marubo Tribe in 2000.

Above: Jeff on a Medical & Evangelism Trip to Romania in 1994. The team visited mountain villages and orphanages.

Below: Jeff's next Trip to Romania in 1998
The team took in humanitarian aid for orphans.

1992 Bibles to Russia Mission Trip with Milk & Honey Ministries - Jeff with Russian Sailors & Children

Ministry in Canada – provides Jeff with fond memories of saints at Grace Bible Chapel, Strasbourg Bible Camp, Schumacher Public School, Timmins Trinity Christian School, Matheson Gospel Chapel and Cochron Gospel Chapel. (Locations in Moosejaw, Saskatchewan and Timmins, Ontario)

Jeff's ministry has blessed his life with **precious friends** from Camps, Churches, Schools, Jail/Bootcamp, Mission Trips, Recovery & Alternative Programs and Outreach. He is especially fond of young people. Jeff recalls one of his mentors, William MacDonald, teaching him a good lesson, "When feeding the flock, put the food down low where the lambs can get it, it won't hurt the sheep to bend over."

Jeff's Bio...

Jeff Tichelar (left) with Dr. Rob Lindsted of Milk & Honey Ministries/Bible Truth in Prophecy, at the Midwest Hebrew Ministries 38th Annual Fall Conference.

Jeff has been commended to the Lord's work for over 35 years and since 2007 by Woodside Bible Chapel in Maywood, IL. Jeff founded a ministry outreach in 2005 at the Riverdale Marina, called "Riverdale Fellowship" where he spoke every Sunday for 6 years until the Marina closed. He also serves as a chaplain for a Christian Motorcycle Club called, "Soldiers of Christ."

Jeff attended the Discipleship Intern Training Program (D.I.T.P.) in San Leandro, CA in 1985-86 where he had the privilege to study under Mr. William MacDonald, Jean Gibson, Carl Knott & Don Robertson.

Jeff spent 17 years as a full-time minister at Oak Lawn Bible Chapel from 1987-2004. He has a real burden for evangelism and has been privileged to use his gifts throughout the United States and Canada. Jeff's interest in Missions has been greatly influenced by his mentor and friend Dr. Rob Lindsted. He has shared the love of Christ in Ecuador, Romania, Russia and Brazil (in the Amazon Jungle).

Jeff has also served for more than 30 years as an Auxiliary Chaplain in the Cook County Sheriff's Department Boot Camp and as in instructor in the "Life Learning Program" at the Cook County Jail. He also began a ministry in 2000 that he calls "Nature Talks" and has been preaching on this theme ever since.

MY PRAYER, THAT OUR LORD WILL BLESS, PROTECT AND WATCH OVER ALL
WHO HEAR MY MESSAGES AND READ MY BOOKS.....AMEN